The SWOT Analysis

Using your Strength to overcome Weaknesses, using Opportunities to overcome Threats

by

Lawrence G Fine

The SWOT Analysis
Copyright © 2010 by Kick It, LLC

Table of Contents

Introduction

SWOT is an acronym which stands for Strength; Weakness; Opportunity and Threats.

SWOT is used to make important decisions. There are times when we have to make a quick judgment, and we will base those decisions on the information we have available. There are other times when we have to look at lots of different factors available, and this is one of the times when we need to use a SWOT analysis.

Many people wrongly assume a SWOT analysis is only relevant for businesses, but it can be invaluable for individuals, organizations and even for team building.

There is another benefit from completing a SWOT analysis, and this is when you complete the analysis on your competitors. The power of the SWOT analysis can change your life.

Before embarking on a SWOT analysis, you should understand this is only a tool -- but it is a powerful tool when used it correctly.

Imagine for a moment, what it would be like if you were able to use SWOT for every business decision you have to make. When you are faced with the need to dig deep, you will discover where your company is today, and be able to make an informed decision for any changes your business needs to make.

Even though it doesn't guarantee 100% success, you'll find your business will be run from a position of strength.

The result of your SWOT analysis is to see the reality of your business or ideas. It will also give you a list of action points - which you should follow, or in some cases – things your company should avoid.

The History of SWOT

The problem faced by many companies is failure. This thought could have been penned in the 21st Century, but it was written and discussed in the mid 20th Century. As companies were failing, people started to ask questions to see if there was a common theme -- many have failed from a lack of planning.

Knowing why the planning had failed was only part of the puzzle; the companies also needed to know what could be done to change failure into success. Businesses would depend on this research to be able to analyze what was happening to their company.

It was a very important matter -- the research was funded by Fortune 500 companies. This should tell us something about our businesses today: if Fortune 500 companies use SWOT, then it should be important for any company.

This research was conducted at Stanford Research Institute; the study took 10 years from 1960 – 1970. The members of the research team were Dr Otis Benepe; Marion Dosher; Albert Humphrey; Birger Lie and Robert Stewart.

Even though companies had corporate planning managers, they discovered a problem: their planning wasn't working -- or rather, the way the planning was being implemented wasn't working.

Companies were spending a lot of money paying these managers, and they didn't see the dividends from their investments. They did what all good companies do; they took a look at what was happening in their business. Not only did they look at the problems, but they made the decision to change. They knew if they didn't act on the results of the research and make some major changes then their companies would also fail.

Like any big corporation or business you have to get people to work as a team, and the planners had to ensure the managers of different departments took action on the advice given.

Seven Key Findings

There were seven key findings by the research group:

- Values
- Appraise
- Motivation
- Search
- Select
- Program
- Act

When this presentation was given in 1964 it was changed from SOFT to SWOT analysis. SOFT meant Satisfactory; Opportunity; Fault and Threat. SWOT means Strength; Weakness; Opportunity and Threats.

Six Questions to Be Answered

SWOT was then taken to the UK and questions were asked. Once these questions had been identified, it was a logical step to analyze what was then needed to see each step completed in the best way possible.

The research team then worked and ended with a 17 step process for planners to follow. A trial was completed in the UK, and then a merger of CWS and J W French Ltd using the SWOT analysis. This proved to be successful, and SWOT has been in use ever since.

These questions are crucial even today in business, and should be the starting point when looking at either a new product, or to see how to improve the net profit for a company or organization.

- What product/s are we selling?
- What is the process we have in place to sell the product?
- Who are our customers, who are going to be interested in our product?
- What ways can we deliver the product to the customers?
- What are the finances needed to create and sell this product?
- Who will oversee all the stages from having an idea, to having enough finance to complete the task?

SWOT in 2008 and Beyond

As we have looked at the history of SWOT, it is worth pausing for a moment, to look at the current financial situation of the world. 2008/2009 saw the world plummet into a major recession. Many financial institutions and major corporations were suddenly facing a financial crisis they hadn't considered possible.

Time could be spent looking at what went wrong, but such an exercise is only valuable if lessons are learned from it, and changes are made to stop it from happening again.

We find there is nothing new in the world. Yes, technology changes, -- but the basic principles of business and life remain very much the same.

As we look at today's corporations, we find many companies have failed from a lack of planning. This is nothing new, because this is exactly the reason the original research was done in the first place -- to discover why corporate planning has failed.

What Is SWOT?

SWOT stands for Strength; Weakness; Opportunity and Threats.

SWOT is use to assess a business or a proposition. This shouldn't be restricted to a business you own, but also to use it for your competitor's business.

When you first look at SWOT it might seem to be simple, and yet the analysis for many people is far from simple. Many people have discovered how difficult it is to complete a project, and find they have no option but to quit trying to complete it. There is another option, and that is to work through the problems, and complete it.

If you want to progress, completing a SWOT analysis is something you should do.

SWOT Analysis

You'll find a SWOT analysis will provide you with a good foundation for your strategy, business proposition, the position of your company, the direction of your company, and even discover which ideas are worth pursuing.

As we have said, SWOT is simple, and can be completed by every business and organizations. You might decide it is an ideal subject for your workshops.

One of the problems a business faces is the reality of where their business is today. Nobody wants to be told that something they have worked hard for is failing, or a skill they thought they had is non-existent.

When you have a brainstorming meeting, you will find the benefit of incorporating SWOT analysis into your discussion.

You will find using SWOT will put the information into a logical order, and this will then help you understand your company, and also the ideas you are considering.

You will make decisions based on the results of the SWOT which is why a lot of people find it difficult to complete the program. These are people who make their decisions based on what they have always done. Or they rely on their instincts -- which can be beneficial, but sometimes we need to have the checks and balances in place.

When Can You Use SWOT in Your Business?

Before you start a business, you should consider completing a SWOT analysis. If you plan on buying a business, use the SWOT analysis to answer various questions you will have regarding the running of the business, and the profitability of the business.

You will find the benefits mostly when writing a business plan. It should also be included in all your strategic planning.

Have you ever considered using SWOT to look at your competitors? It is an exercise which will prove to be profitable to your business, if you act on the results.

Marketing is an area which many people are not experts in, but you can take your marketing to a new level, when you add SWOT into your thinking.

You will discover how business never stays static. The business should either be moving forward, or the business will be moving backwards. Just look at companies who refuse to move forward with the changes in the way people shop, and see how many stores on the "High Street" are now closed. As you look to change your business or create a new product, a SWOT analysis is imperative to ensure you don't waste time and energy on a product which isn't needed or wanted in the marketplace.

For businesses who are involved in research, a SWOT analysis again is crucial as the results are recorded and "White Papers" are written.

Questions to ask when preparing to complete SWOT

We saw earlier in the book that the research team identified some questions, and these questions will enable you to turn your SWOT analysis into action.

Let's remind ourselves of the questions.
- What product/s are we selling?
- What is the process we have in place to sell the product?
- Who are the customers, who are the people interested in our product?
- What ways can we deliver the product to the customers?
- What are the finances needed to create and sell this product?
- Who will oversee all the stages from having an idea, to having enough finance to complete the task?

How do you put your answers to these questions into action? You should keep these questions in mind, as you prepare to complete your SWOT analysis.

What product/s are we selling?

If you are going to start a business or already have a business it is important to know what product or service you are going to be selling.

Because it is easy and cheap to start a business online, many people struggle with conceptualizing what they are going to sell. They will ask dozens of people for a product or service they can sell, and like any survey completed with a random set of people, you will get lots of different answers.

If you can't decide on a product then you won't be able to answer the other questions, so you should use your SWOT analysis to find a good product or service to sell.

What is the process we have in place to sell the product?

Or to put it simply, how are we selling our product? Today, there are so many different choices: do you sell it online, offline, or both?

If you are selling the product offline, do you need premises to sell from or can you use your home? If you sell online, what type of website do you need? How will you process payments for the products? How many staff will you need to employ?

Who are the customers, who are the people interested in our product?

As you develop your business you will see who the core group of people who are interested in the products being sold.

You might develop a product which is targeted to women in their early 20's. Now it doesn't mean only women will buy, because you could have a spouse, parent, sibling or friend who would want to make a purchase for a gift.

When you look at your customer base, remember all the different groups of people who will be interested in buying your product.

What ways can we deliver the product to the customers?

Delivery of your products is very important, and from a business perspective you need to know exactly the costs involved for making deliveries. If you are going to offer the product overseas, how much will it cost you to send it? Would a customer be prepared to pay a $50 shipping cost on a product which is selling for $60?

People usually are only prepared to pay high shipping costs, when what they are purchasing is a product they have to have and are unable to buy locally.

How can you take advantage of people around the world who are desperate for your product? Which options are there for delivering it at a cheaper price?

What are the finances needed to create and sell this product?

This is an area which can make or break a business. You need to know your actual costs before you start to price a product. Ensure you have an accurate projection before you start to create any new product. You might think you can sell a product for $10 but when you break down all the costs involved in creating the product you discover the product can't be produced for less than $15. This is time to re-evaluate your product and pricing strategy.

Yes, there are times when you need a loss leader, but any business will tell you they have products which have huge ROI.

What investment will be needed to create and sell your product? Finance is an important part of your business, start with the right information and take time to really look at this aspect of your company.

Who will oversee all the stages from having an idea, to having enough finance to complete the task?

When you have an idea, it can take time before the idea becomes a reality. There are various stages to consider and costs which are needed as part of the process. You can guess what the costs are, but nothing can be more disheartening than not being able to complete a task because you've run out of financing.

You will need a manager who will oversee the whole business. Now, the manager might be yourself, but you might need to employ a general manager to do the work. Departments need to work together, people need to know what is happening, and this is something you might not have time to do.

Ensuring everybody is on the same page at the same time is crucial for the success of a business. Look at your SWOT analysis in light of this.

These are the six important questions that need to be asked and answered every time you make a major change to your business or introduce a new product or service.

SWOT Analysis Template

Before we can look into the details of the different elements of a SWOT analysis, we need to understand the basics of the template. The basic template won't change, yet the questions asked can and should be relevant to the situation. It is important to understand what has caused a company or individual to undertake the task of completing the analysis.

The template normally used is in a grid format, and would look like the one below. It should always include the subject. You can then have a list of questions in each section and an area to answer the questions. There is no limit to the number of questions and answers you have, but more in-depth questions will give you a superior result.

The challenge is to use the template to stimulate healthy discussion. This is the time for egos to be left outside the room. Considet this: a member of the staff might have a different perspective on the way the company is operating. They might see a weakness or a threat where the management does not. When a number of people are involved in a business, more people can cover more problem areas.

Example

We will look at a simple example, but you can use the principle for any area of your business.

Imagine you want a new design for your business card, and this is passed to a member of staff. Now, this isn't a big project, but what will happen if the person you gave it to was not able to design anything? A job which should take a few hours could take weeks as the person looks at a blank piece of paper wondering where to start. Someone from the design department finally sees the problem, and immediately helps out by designing the new business card in the staff member's place.

A task becomes a problem in the hands of the wrong person, and this is exactly why the right people should be given jobs they are best at. It is a case of not putting square pegs into round holes.

SWOT Analysis Sample Template

This is only a sample template, although some examples of the criteria you should be looking at when personalizing your own SWOT analysis template are listed below.

Subject of SWOT Analysis	
It is important that everybody involved knows the reasons for completing the analysis.	
Strengths	**Weaknesses**
• Advantages of	• Disadvantages of

proposition?

- Capabilities?
- Competitive advantages?
- USP?
- Resources, Assets, People?
- Experience, knowledge, data?
- Financial reserves, likely returns?
- Marketing - reach, distribution, awareness?
- Innovative aspects?
- Location and geographical?
- Price, value, quality?
- Accreditations, qualifications, certifications?

proposition?

- Gaps in capabilities?
- Lack of competitive strength?
- Reputation, presence and reach?
- Financials?
- Own known vulnerabilities?
- Timescales, deadlines and pressures?
- Cash flow, start-up cash-drain?
- Continuity, supply chain robustness?
- Effects on core activities, distraction?
- Reliability of data, plan predictability?
- Morale, commitment,

• Processes, systems, IT, communications?	leadership?
	• Accreditations, etc?
• Cultural, attitudinal, behavioral?	• Processes and systems, etc?
• Management cover, succession?	• Management cover, succession?
• Philosophy and values?	

Opportunities	**Threats**
• Market developments?	• Political effects?
	• Legislative effects?
• Competitors' vulnerabilities?	• Environmental effects?
• Industry or lifestyle trends?	• IT developments?
	• Competitor intentions - various?
• Technology development and innovation?	• Market demand?
	• New technologies, services, ideas?
• Global influences?	
• New markets, vertical, horizontal?	• Vital contracts and partners?

- Niche target markets?
- Geographical, export, import?
- New USP?
- Tactics: e.g., surprise, major contracts?
- Business and product development?
- Information and research?
- Partnerships, agencies, distribution?
- Volumes, production, economies?
- Seasonal, weather, fashion influences?

- Sustaining internal capabilities?
- Obstacles faced?
- Insurmountable weaknesses?
- Loss of key staff?
- Sustainable financial backing?
- Economy - home, abroad?
- Seasonality, weather effects?

Subject of SWOT Analysis

The first stage of completing a SWOT analysis is to know exactly the subject for this analysis.

If you don't explain the reason for completing the analysis, you will find different people in your company or organization will come out with different responses.

In certain situations there will be people who will receive a copy of the completed SWOT analysis. If they don't know the reason for the assessment, the results will be meaningless for them.

Imagine for a moment, a person decides to start a business. They complete a SWOT analysis, and then ask a "Third Party" to review it, and to give their views on the results. But, without a clear vision of what the person wants to achieve, the "Third Party" could make suggestions which could be detrimental to the new business.

Like anything in life, we need to be able to communicate clearly what the plan and goals are. Once they have been ascertained, then people can read and make suggestions of the way forward.

It doesn't matter whether the world is in a recession or has come out of a recession. Companies may be hiring rather than firing staff, companies may be making a profit rather than a loss – but there are certain subjects which can be relevant at any time when doing business.

A Company, Business or Organization

As you look at your company, business or organization, you need to discover your exact position in the market.

If you decide to enter a market which already has a recognized company or companies, you'll need to determine where you will fit into that market.

When you analyze the market, you will find different companies are marketing to a different group of people. This is crucial to know, because if you enter an oversaturated market, then you are more likely to fail. Should you target an area that other companies are ignoring? If they have discovered that people in this market do not spend money on consumer goods, then again you are most likely to fail.

A Business Idea

You have a great idea, or you believe it is a great idea, but unless you research it and use your SWOT analysis you won't know how well it will be accepted in the marketplace.

Keep in mind that completing a SWOT analysis doesn't mean your idea will be the next big thing – however, it will ensure that at the very least, your idea is feasible.

A New Product

You've discovered the need for a new product to be released by your company or business, and a SWOT analysis will enable you to check up on the competition or to see if there is any at all.

Buying a Company or Even an Asset for Your Company

You have decided owning another company is the next project for your company. However, before spending major cash you should always do a SWOT analysis to complement the financial statements available.

If you are looking to buy assets for the company again a SWOT analysis will help you making the decision needed.

Becoming a Partner in a Business

There will be occasions when you need to work with someone, and when the time comes you need to decide whether you can both benefit from making a partnership. Using a SWOT analysis will allow you to see exactly what both parties are offering as the two businesses become one.

There are many times when a business will require a SWOT analysis to be initiated. But, like all lists ours isn't definitive, because there are times when you have a unique reason or situation for completing it.

Strength

For Business

The strength of a company, business or organization will change as more and more people get involved with the work. This is the main reason it is imperative to go back to your SWOT analysis to ensure it is up-to-date.

When you start a business, your strengths might only be what you are able to do, but as more and more people get involved, you will find your list of strengths enlarging.

However, the whole purpose of completing a SWOT analysis for a business is to see whether your product or service is going to be viable and give you a net profit which is sustainable over many years.

What strengths does your business have? If you are not sure, then take time to look and see what you are doing right in your business.

Maybe, you have only just started and you're offering a service. What is the feedback your customers or clients are giving? Are they all saying the same thing, highlight one aspect of your service? This is a great strength and one you need to examine to see if you can improve or even offer a better service. The same is true if you are selling a product: listen to what the customer is saying.

Often the customer will give feedback on an area of our business which you had not initially considered.

When you start to list your strengths, do not give in to the temptation is to stop before you have completed it. The reason is simple: we don't want to sound like we are bragging.

However, it isn't bragging -- it is a way to find out how you can improve your business.

Strength Example

You might be selling motorbikes, which started because you have a passion for bikes. Maybe, you were a teen who bought their first bike, but couldn't afford the maintenance bills which came with it. This spurred you on to complete a maintenance course, and now you can talk to your customers about how they can do their own repairs to their bikes. You might even go and do a small repair for your customers. You don't think of it as a service, because you do it while you are chatting with them. But the customer comes back time and time again, because they know you will help them when the bike has a problem.

Look at your business and see all the ways you help people, especially the ways you don't charge people for your time and knowledge. These are strengths which we often don't see, because they are something we do without being asked.

How Do International Companies Promote Their Strengths

Now is the time to look at your product/service and compare it to your competition. This isn't the time to say, "XXX Company's product is the biggest load of rubbish you will ever buy." If you do, then you will guarantee people will start to say the same thing about your product or company.

We all know the international products which are on our television screens. They all have one thing in common: they play to their strengths. Remember the advert about a certain battery company, they show their competitors as a battery which runs out of power sooner than theirs does. Their strength is their battery lasts longer.

Watch the different advertising campaigns to see how companies portray their strengths, and see how you can do the same thing with your product/service.

Questions to Ask About Your Product or Service

It is time to breakdown every aspect of your business, and to find the strengths you have in each area. This is a reason why many larger companies have departments, and within a department certain members of staff are designated specific jobs. When you are the sole employee or are a one-person company, then it is harder to do this because you have to be a "Jack of All Trades."

Remember the task at hand is not to discourage you, but to find those strengths which often lie hidden.

Regardless of the size of your business, one of your strengths should always be reliability and quality.

People starting out in business often fail with pricing their services or products. They see someone selling cheap products and think there is no market for something which is more expensive.

If you believe this to be true, take a look at your High Street and see the Dollar Shops alongside those who have higher prices. The strength often of the higher price stores is in the quality of their products.

You should discover what strengths your competition is offering, and then see what your strength is. Are they different? If you say, "Yes, they are very different," then you should be marketing your strength.

Look at the experience of the end-user, have you considered this, and what strength have you put into the experience for them.

What are the strengths of your customer services? Do you have a customer service policy?

Yes, you need to know the strengths of your competition, but most importantly you must know the strength of your company and products.

For Personal

This can be a difficult exercise for many people, because they live thinking and seeing the negative in every situation. While this might be good at times, it does restrict how a person works and reacts.

Pride is two sided. Many don't want to talk about their strengths, because they don't want to be seen to be prideful. They will say "I'm no good at this," while hoping someone else will say "No, you are really good at it."

This is the time to start listing down all the skills you have. What did you learn in school which is a strength you use all the time?

Remember to include all the skills you use at work, especially if a certain task is always assigned to you. If you look carefully, you will see how other people have recognized these strengths in you.

Have you considered as one of your strengths your list of contacts? There will be times when you can't help a person with your skills, but you can help them by putting them in contact with someone you know.

Without boasting, what are you able to do which is better than anyone else? How many times have you looked at a business or even a hobby, and think it would be better if the way it was completed was changed? You might be someone who can see the bigger picture, and this is a strength many businesses today are looking for.

Do you have any resources available which will enable you to act from a position of strength? You might use a certain product or employ a

certain method which could be used to help
other people.

One resource which many people wish they had
a lot of is "time." Imagine if you are out of work,
retired or work part-time, you have a car and
can use it as a hospital car or a charity. Time is
a valuable commodity which many people don't
have.

Another strength which a lot of people would
love to have is "patience". Are you patient and
can spend hours and hours teaching the same
thing to one person? There are people with
learning difficulties who would love someone to
explain a problem in simple terms, and be
prepared to teach it over and over until they
have grasped it.

Don't overlook anything on your list, because
you will find the greatest strength is something
you don't necessarily see as strength.

If possible, ask other people what they see as your strengths. A good test is to ask a number of people to list your strengths, and then to compare the lists to see if there are any strengths listed by a good number of people. The secret here is to be as objective as possible. If you don't know where to start, try compiling a list of your characteristics. Not all your characteristics are strengths but some will be.

Summary

- Examine your business for its strengths.
- Examine any product and service you sell.
- Examine your competitor to see what their strengths are.
- Examine your personal life for your strengths
- Remember to include you resources, contact and character.

Weakness

For Business

When you look for the weaknesses in your business, some will be obvious yet others you will try and justify by saying, "They are not really a weakness, when I have the time/patience/funds/resources to deal with it then this will be sorted out."

Let's be realistic here, a weakness exists and it is for the good of your company to recognize them, so that you may be able to see how to deal with it.

Let's take a very basic example, you want to design a logo for your company but you have no design skills. This is a weakness for your business, unless you have a person employed with design skills. But, your company is small, and the business model doesn't warrant a full time designer on the payroll.

You could say this will be sorted when the business grows and I can employ a full time designer. But what if the business is such you can never justify a full time salary for a designer.

You have a choice to make, admit it is a weakness, and that you will either outsource it to a designer or decide you don't need a logo and remove it from your "To Do List."

Is a weakness as big a problem as people think? Not really -- you can either look at how you can turn a weakness into a strength, or decide that an area of your business isn't worth pursuing.

Imagine for a moment you are considering investing into a company, when you know what the weaknesses are you can make a clear decision whether to invest or to say no this time.

For the moment, go through all your products and also your business model. Just like your previous task of finding your strengths, now look for your weaknesses.

Some areas of weakness within your business will be easy to find, but others you will need to dig deep.

Do you remember how we looked at some international companies to see how they highlight their strengths to you? Now go and look at the same companies and see what do to limit the negative effects of their weaknesses. They might hint at some of them, but normally they are busy turning anything negative into a positive.

The one thing you can't afford here is to look at the weaknesses and think your business will never flourish; being able to look at a weakness positively is also a strength.

How many times have you read about people who are trying to start out in business and all list all the things they can't do? They not only list them, they also normally cannot see a way around these obstacles.

Let's say you are a writer and you have written a best selling book, a publishing house thinks this is a perfect match for a Spanish market. They want you to translate the book. Now, the problem you have is you don't speak Spanish. This is a weakness for your business. You can either refuse to do it because you can't do it yourself, or you can hire a translator or translating company to do the work for you.

A weakness will normally have two solutions for you to follow. One will be a way to turn the weakness into strength; the other is an exit plan.

If you are a start-up business then you won't have a list of buyers, and normally you don't know how many people will buy from you.

If your business suddenly expands, are you going to be able to cope with the extra work, or will you need to employ more people?

Many new businesses can get into the vicious circle of seeing themselves as the new business or have an inferiority complex because they are not as well known as the bigger companies in town. If this is how you perceive your business, then you will convey this impression to others through what you do and what you say.

Information is readily available through the web these days, and people will be able to discover what you think and say. Turning this around will mean guarding what you say and communicate online.

For Personal

This is even tougher than trying to see the weakness in your business. You might be someone who has been told how useless you are, or you that will never amount to anything. This is so ingrained in your thinking; you will not see anything as a weakness, but part of your character which can never be changed. This isn't true, and you can become a stronger person. You can take back control of your life.

It's time to get practical now. Look at your life and start to list all the things you want to improve. You might not have all the solutions right now to see this happen, but the first step is to create a list.

When a person has an addiction, they know they should avoid it. Is someone knows and admits to having an addiction then they know what to do. But, what about people who might not have an addiction, but know that certain things are not good for them? These are the things we need to focus on.

You know that eating certain foods at mid-day will cause you to feel drowsy for the rest of the day. If your work means you have to be alert, then the simple answer is to avoid the food. For some people eating a simple food like pasta will cause this reaction, and a change in diet is needed.

Again, ask your friends and family what they see as a weakness in your life. Tell them why you are asking, and don't accept those comments where people are finding fault in every thing you do. You are not looking for just negative statement, because you want to improve your life for the better.

You need to remember we are not all good at everything, and you will find you can't do everything and do them well.

The saying "The truth hurts," is one you are going to face now. People might want to say nice things to you, but when they are asked to be specific, they will say things which could hurt you.

You might have heard comments in the past, but you thought they were being mean-spirited, but now is the time to face the hard realities of what is happening. It is time to consider how much truth is being spoken, and how much you want to embrace the truth.

Learn to discern between someone telling you a truth with a right attitude in their speech, from someone telling you a truth but with anger, hate, or disdain in their hearts. When someone is angry, it is hard to appreciate any glimmer of truth in their statement.

Realize your ego is going to be attacked during this exercise, but also realize you are going to come out of this as a stronger person.

Summary

- Examine your business for any weakness.
- Examine any product and service you sell.
- Examine your competitor to see what their weakness is.
- Examine your personal life for any weakness you might have.

- Ask friends and family to tell you which weakness in your life they see.

Opportunity

For Business

There are opportunities all around us, but so often we miss them because we are too focused on the negative aspects of life.

When there is a world recession, at some stage the world and its major countries will come out of it, and people will spend money again. How can you use your time now to develop something which will be needed when the recession ends?

How can you develop a product or service based on a frustration you are facing today? Maybe you needed a service or product, and have spent hours trying to find it online, but cannot find it. As you look at the problems you faced, you could also be looking at the opportunities which are around.

Negativity is one side of the coin, and every problem will have at least one solution. You might see something other people have missed. Take your opportunities and start to see which way you business can move forward.

This is a good time to look at your current products or services and see how you can improve them. Are there any opportunities to develop your product or service for the overseas market?

When you looked at your competitors did you find their products were of an inferior quality to yours? How can you take advantage of this knowledge and use it for your business without saying bad things about the other companies?

When we look for opportunities we will find them all around us. The question is: are you prepared to use these opportunities, or will you be thinking, "I thought up that idea and could have made a fortune if I developed it."?

Opportunities need to be acted on, look at the ones which are relevant to your business, and see what action you can take for them.

For Personal

In your personal life, you will find opportunities are also all around you, but again you need to identify the relevant ones and then take action.

What are the opportunities which you face, are you aware of them all? It's time to make a list and see what is happening in your life.

Trends come and go, but if you watch them you will see how these will open up different opportunities for you.

Technology is an area which is always changing, are you aware of any opportunities which you can take from your knowledge or experience?

As you look at the broader picture of your SWOT analysis, are there any strengths or weaknesses which you can use as an opportunity as well?

Going back to the example of the motor bike seller, who has extensive knowledge about maintenance, could they have an opportunity to open a cheap repair shop to help other bike owners? Could they pass on their knowledge by running some workshops to teach other bike owners how to do their own basic repairs?

When a person looks for opportunities in life they can find them. Start to see what is available for you.

Summary

- Examine your business for any opportunities which may arise.
- Examine any product and service you sell to see what new opportunities are arising for changes in the business world.
- Examine your competitor to see how you can find opportunities from what they are not or even from what they do.
- Examine your personal life for all the different opportunities which are available every day when you look for them.
- Look for opportunities in every situation.

Threat

For Business

This is an area a lot of businesses don't want to consider. They know there are threats all around them, but if they ignore them, then maybe they will no longer exist. Nothing is further from the truth, ignoring a threat means your business will suffer.

Threats come in all shapes and sizes and for businesses it can be something you didn't consider when you had first started.

If you're in the food industry, then legislation can and will impact your business, especially if you're not informed of the changes. The easy solution is to be aware, and have notification of any changes your country makes regarding your industry.

You only have to look in your local
neighborhood to see how many "Mom & Pop"
business have closed because of larger
companies. For some, they didn't take the
threat seriously, and they thought loyalty
would win the day.

The reality is that even their most loyal
customers had less money to spend, so they
went to the bigger stores which would allow
their dollars to go a littler further.

Are there ways to take on the big companies,
which have a lot of money to spend? The
answer is yes, but it takes time to see exactly
where you fit into the niche, but also to know
your USP and to take advantage of it.

Many large companies have seen the threats of
competition and have come up with solutions
which make them stand out from the crowd.
Many smaller companies didn't want to do this

and have lost their business because they don't want to change.

Many businesses will find their income is increased at certain seasons, the food industry will see an increase before Thanksgiving. If this is your niche, how can you do something which the big companies don't offer as a service which will then get people to buy your product as well?

Did you notice we said which service, and you might be thinking you don't offer any services, because you see a product? This might be true, but giving a service could make a difference to the product you sell.

Let's say you sell turkeys for Thanksgiving, one of the highest searches last Thanksgiving was to "how to cook a turkey." Because people are not taught today to cook this is a major problem. People don't always understand the recipes or know ovens can cook at different pressure depending on the usage in an area. Imagine if you offered a simple service where you allowed people to call a dedicated line and got advice on how to cook their turkey. But, you make it a free service for those who have bought from you. That is a simple example but one which could be profitable for a smaller company who want a share of the market.

Another threat for a smaller company is keeping their staff especially if larger companies can pay higher salaries. What can you do about this? Maybe, offer job security, retraining especially if your company has to diversify, employ older people or people who corporations are reluctant to employ.

If you find your key members of staff are being head-hunted, you should look for a solution to keep your key members. Don't think it is part of the business process, but look at what employment package is being offered, and see how much of it you can offer.

If a threat is great enough, you will work to find a counter-solution to the problem. It is when threats happen you have to look closer at your business model, and make any necessary changes.

One of the biggest threats in business is a lack of focus. You'd see the bigger picture rather than focus on the current situation. You are chasing different solutions which might not be needed for a few more years. There is a need for balance here; you need to focus on your current situation as well as on the bigger picture.

People have seen problems with their business, and they immediately closed it down to follow another idea which they think is good. The problem is the new idea hasn't been able to

generate any income, and then the business owner is wondering what to else do. Balance is the key here; don't close one business hoping your new idea will generate bigger returns.
Keep the profitable business running, even if it means running it as a part time business, while you use the rest of your time to develop the new idea.

Social networking is a big threat, and many people are now seeing the problems connected with the use of these sites. People have been using them to say what they really feel about their employer, and generating bad publicity for these companies.

The saying "There is no bad publicity," is false because your reputation can be ruined in seconds -- especially when the publicity can go around the world in seconds as well.
Gone are the days when a local paper might write something negative about a local business

and it stays in the local area. With the Internet, the information can move from a local to a global scale instantly.

Have a plan of action regarding any negative publicity; know how to turn this threat around.

If your small business is going to do something which will affect the income and profit of a large company, they will take the threat seriously, and be looking at ways to counteract it.

Be aware of how this could happen with any changes you make, and know how to deal with the corporations who will have far more experience and money available to deal with these cases.

For Personal

Personal threats can be very different from business threats, but the one thing these will do is stop you reaching your full potential if you don't recognize them and take action.

You might have a job and it might be something you love to do, however, with the changes in technology you need to learn how to use them to see yourself in the same job in twenty years time. Yes, it might be a problem getting used to something you have never used before, but if you can't overcome your fear then you might find yourself without a job soon enough.

Many people love to travel, and for some the idea of going around the world is something they dream of. But, they know they need to have money and also some type of skill to work their way around the world. Some will decide to put their social life on hold while they study to become a TOEFL teacher. So for them the threat is their friends who want them to go out and have fun instead of staying in to hit the books. Again, you can balance the two; maybe you can socialize once a week so that you don't end up acting like a hermit.

What are your dreams? How can you achieve them? What threats will stand in the way of those dreams becoming a reality?

Talk to young people who are taking a gap year, and see how they have sacrificed to see their dreams come true.

If you want to go to remote Africa to help with conservation, what are the obstacles you face? Maybe, the first one is your parents who are concerned about their teenager not only being away from home, but in a remote place where there are no phones or Internet. How do you deal with this? One answer is to get as much information as possible to give to your parents. Another is to talk to people who have been there, and get them to talk to your parents as well. Reassurance is the solution to this obstacle and threat.

Summary

- Examine your business for any threats, and have strategies in place to deal with them.
- Examine any product and service you sell to ensure there are no hidden threats.
- Examine your competitor to see what threats might come from them and be prepared.
- Examine your personal life for any threats which is stopping you realizing your dreams.

Action from Your SWOT Analysis

This is the final stage of your SWOT analysis --but it is an important stage, because you need to take action from all your ground work.

You were presented with a proposition, and you used your SWOT analysis to see what the proposition was really like. You have to remember the person who had the idea will normally see it as one of the greatest ideas around, and they will talk positively about it. As an outsider your job is to remove the emotional aspects, and look in great detail at the idea and proposition.

If you find the proposition is strong, ensure you check all the financial documentation as well, then you are ready to look at the weakness, opportunity and threats before you make a final commitment to the project.

What do you do if you find the idea is in reality very weak, there are problems which the person isn't prepared to accept and make any changes or allowances for? The answer would normally be simple; you do nothing but refuse the proposition. Unless you want to risk your investment ... walking away is the answer.

What did you discover when you completed the SWOT analysis for your personal life? Did you find a way to develop your career, or did it cause you to consider a complete change of career?

You might have dreams and ideas which you would love to pursue but fear has stopped you, but now you have discovered you have all the skills and the opportunity is too good to turn down.

Yes, stepping outside our comfort zone is not a comfortable place to be in, but we can benefit when we do. Often, the fears we have are only in our minds, and they never happen. The SWOT analysis can help you relate to those fears and see ways to eliminate them.

If you have lost your job because of the recession or companies going bankrupt, now is the time to look for all the opportunities around which you have the right skills for.

It is only a small percentage of people who can look at a negative situation, and discover an opportunity waiting for someone to capitalize on. Your SWOT analysis will help you become that person.

If you already own a business, then use your SWOT analysis to see what can be done to make your business better and stronger. Sometimes tough decisions have to be made, and none is tougher than deciding a weakness is best dealt with by removing it from the business life. There are times when you can find a solution to the weakness, but other times it isn't possible. All that happens is the weakness is draining your finances and resources, which could be used in other parts of the business.

It is tough when you have to do this, but it is important to have a well rounded business.

Conclusion

Having now seen the benefits of working through a SWOT analysis, you are left with a decision. Do you do the hard work, and really see your business, organization and even your personal life as it really is?

Yes, it is hard work, but you should remember when problem areas are brought to life you are given another decision to make. Do you ignore the problem, or do you decide to do something which will change them into strengths?

A problem only remains a problem while you do nothing about it. Leaving it buried means that at some stage it will be discovered, and the task of fixing it could be more painful.

Be brave, take a conscious decision to tackle the your problems, and come out with a stronger business or organization -- or even as a stronger person ready to face all the world will throw at you.

Lastly, if something happens that you are not prepared for, you are secure in the knowledge that you with SWOT, you have the tools to examine the situation clearly and turn it around for good.

14185166R00046

Printed in Poland
by Amazon Fulfillment
Poland Sp. z o.o., Wrocław